Incy-Wincy Moo-Cow

a book of
weird and wacky
nursery rhymes

by
John Cunliffe

Illustrated by Jan Barger

MACDONALD YOUNG BOOKS

Incy-Wincy Moo-Cow

Incy-Wincy Moo-Cow,
Climbing up the hill;
Munch grass,
Munch grass,
Eat your fill!

Here comes the farmer,
To make the golden hay;
And all the cows shall munch it,
On a winter day.

Jack and Jill went up the hill

Jack and Jill went up the hill,
but Jack said, "Wait a minute!
If we climb up to find that well,
there might be nothing in it!"

So they turned themselves about,
and went to the corner shop;
where they bought a bottle of lemonade,
and a can of fizzy pop.

Little Bo Peep has gone to sleep

"I can't sleep," said Little Bo Peep,
So, mother said, "Just count your sheep;
Count them fast and count them quick;
Count them swift and count them slick."

The sheep jumped over the meadow wall,
And Bo Peep tried to count them all;
The sheep, they came so fast and free,
That she could never rightly see,
Where one sheep ended – the next began,
In such a woolly blur they ran;

And then she saw the open gate,
Alas, alack, it was too late;
The sheep ran away over the hill,
And as far as I know they're running still;
All were lost, for ever, it seems,
In the drowsy drift of dreams.

Bo Peep slept until the day,
When all her dreams were fled away.
Father said, "Did you have a good sleep?"
"Yes," she said, "I counted sheep."

Ride a clock-horse

Ride a clock-horse,
To bilberry pie,
To see the old moon-man,
Up in the sky.

He shall have sing-song,
Wherever he goes,
With moonshine and star-dust,
To tickle his toes.

Hey Diddle Diddle

Hey Diddle Diddle,
The cat and the fiddle,
The rocket went round the moon;
The astronauts laughed to see such fun,
And said, "We'll be coming home soon."

Little Boy Blue

Little Boy Blue
switch on your computer;
the sheep in the meadow
are riding your scooter;
the cows in the corn
are all cybernetic;
and the electric-hens
are looking pathetic;
they're laying square eggs
that no one will eat,
and the weather-control
has turned up the heat.

Little Boy Blue
there's no time to sleep;
the computerized farm
has schedules to keep;
so, Little Boy Blue
just switch on your screen;
the sheep-organizer;
the egg-machine...
The clocks they are ticking
all night and all day;
there's no time for taking
a snooze in the hay!

Little Polly Flinders

Little Polly Flinders
Sat by the gas fire,
Warming her pretty little toes.

Then the fire went out,
And... poor little lass,
She had no money
To put into the gas...

She was frozen
To the tip of her nose!

Mary Muffet

Mary Muffet sat on the sofa,
Watching the old TV;
There came down a spider,
Who sat down beside her,
To see what he could see.

"I'm not scared of you!" she said,
The spider gave never a peep;
She snipped away his spider thread,
But he was fast asleep.

I love little dinosaur

I love little dinosaur,
his horns are so sharp;
and if I don't hurt him,
he'll gobble me up.

So I'll not pull his tail,
or drive him away,
but Dino and I
so gently will play.

The new adventures of Humpty Dumpty

Humpty Dumpty
Said "I don't dare,
To sit on a wall,"
So he sat on a chair.
He didn't fall,
And he didn't crack,
So the king's men took
Their horses back.

They all went home,
To have their tea,
And watch the films,
On the old TV.

Humpty Dumpty
Sat on a wall,
Knitting a pair
Of socks;
He fell down,
And broke his crown,
Upon a pile of rocks.

Humpty Dumpty
Sat on a wall,
To watch
A football match;
He shouted and cheered,
Till he tumbled off,
And fell in
A strawberry patch!

Humpty Dumpty
Sat on a wall,
Humpty Dumpty
Had a great fall;
The king's men said,
"We know what to do."
And they stuck him together
With Superglue.

Humpty Dumpty
Sat on a box,
Mending his
Aunt Matilda's socks;
"Good egg!" she said,
"That's really neat!"
And put the socks
Upon her feet.

Humpty Dumpty
Sat on a wall;
Humpty Dumpty
Had a great fall;
He didn't break at all,
He was hard-boiled!

The Grand Old Duke of Pisa

The Grand Old Duke of Pisa,
He had ten thousand peas;
He rolled them up and down the hill,
As often as he did please;
And when they were up they were up,
And when they were down they were down,
And when they were only half-way up...

...they were reduced to pease-pudding, which he put in little bowls
and gave to hungry people in the town.

Dr Foster

Dr Foster went to Gloucester,
on an electric train;
the train was late,
and he got in a state,
and never went there again.

Ten floppy disks

Ten floppy disks,
Looking quite fine;
One touched a magnet,
And then there were nine.

Nine floppy disks,
Going out of date;
One got corrupted,
And then there were eight.

Eight floppy disks,
In computer heaven;
One was left in the sun,
And then there were seven.

Seven floppy disks,
Storing funny pics;
Someone spilt his coffee,
And then there were six.

Six floppy disks,
That surely looked live;
One jammed in the slot,
And then there were five.

Five floppy disks,
Dropped behind the door;
One got stepped on,
And then there were four.

Four floppy disks,
Taken down to tea;
One got toasted,
And then there were three.

Three floppy disks,
Taken to the zoo;
One fell in the pig-food,
And then there were two.

Two floppy disks,
Got sat upon;
One cracked in two,
And then there was one.

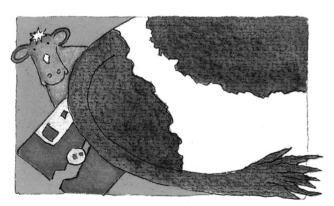

One floppy disk,
The very last one!
Was lost on the bus,
And then there were none!

Moo, moo, white cow

Moo, moo, white cow,
have you any butter?

I might give you some,
if you don't mutter!

Prate, prate foolish child,
Butter you must earn;
Take my milk and put it in a churn.

Churn it up – churn it up,
For an hour or two,
Pitter-pat, pitter-pat,
There's a pat for you.

Sing a song of half a shilling

Sing a song of half a shilling,
I'd bake a pie and be quite willing,
to fill it with a fruity filling,
berries, currants, things like that,
but never wing of bird or bat;
I'd rather bake it in my hat,
so it might hold no living thing
that might squeak, or squawk or sing;
and I would never think of rye,
to make a crust for such a pie;
it wouldn't hold
it wouldn't rise,
it wouldn't be a nice surprise,
for any king
that you might find,
with pie-and-custard
on his mind.

Robin and Bobbin

Robin and Bobbin, two big-bellied men,
Went to Weight Watchers, now and then;
They ate an elephant and two fat whales;
Their wives said, "Oh! You'll bust the scales!
You're supposed to be slimming – this just won't do!"
So they went down to London, and swallowed the zoo.

Little Jack Horner

Little Jack Horner,
Sat in a corner,
No wonder he grew up strange;
He ate his dinner with the cat,
And his tea at the kitchen range;

He had his breakfast at bedtime,
His supper at crack of dawn,
His lunch he ate at the top of a tree,
Elevenses on the lawn.

Hickory Dickory – *what?*

Hickory Dickory – *what?*
Some nonsense about a mouse running up a clock.
Well, I've looked at the clocks in our house,
and no way can I imagine one with an up-running mouse.
Take the digital clock on the new cooker –
Now that's a real high-tech looker!
But it's all shiny chrome and plastic,
No foothold for a mouse,
no matter how gymnastic.
There's another on the video,
and one on the telly,
They'd make a scrabbling mouse,
look a proper Nelly.

There's an alarm clock by my bed;
Now, if a mouse took it into its head,
To run over it or round it,
It could jump it or bound it,
and it might jump on the bell
and sound it;
But running *up* it would be a different matter,
It would fall off the table with a clatter.

To bring old Hickory up to our time,
there's no place at all for a mouse in that rhyme.

Little Jack Horner... and his mother

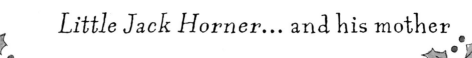

Little Jack Horner,
sat in the corner...

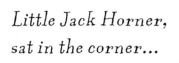

Your name isn't Horner at all,
You've just put that in to make it rhyme!

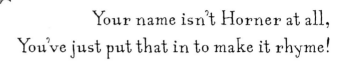

Little Jack Abel,
Sat in the corner...

...and what are you doing, sitting in a corner to eat?
Sit at the table, properly, for your dinner!

Little Jack Abel,
Sat at the table,
Eating a Christmas pie...

It is *not* a pie; it's a flan!

Little Jack Abel,
Sat at the table,
Eating a Christmas flan...

It isn't Christmas, either!

Little Jack Abel,
Sat at the table,
Eating a midsummer flan;
He put in his thumb...

Disgusting child! Use your spoon!
We do not put thumbs in our dinner!

Little Jack Abel,
Sat at the table,
Eating a midsummer flan;
He put in his spoon,
And pulled out a plum...

And how can you pull a plum
out of a strawberry flan?
Anyway, it doesn't rhyme!

Little Jack Abel,
Sat at the table,
Eating a midsummer flan;
He put in his spoon,
And pulled out a prune...

Wrong again, even if it does rhyme!
This is a *strawberry* flan !

Little Jack Abel,
Sat at the table,
Eating a midsummer flan;
He put in his spoon,
Like a funny buffoon,

And ate three strawberries, and quickly,
Before his mother could get another word in,
He slipped in the final rhyme...

And said, "What a good boy I am!"

Mary had a little cow

Mary had a little cow,
Its milk came fast and free,
She milked it morning, noon and night,
And put it in her tea.

The milk, I mean,
Not the cow,
It never would fit in;
And if she could have squashed it down,
It would have been a sin.
No matter what the size of cup,
The cow would surely fill it up!
And how to get the sugar stirred?
It surely would be quite absurd;
She might have tried to use its tail
To whisk it round and round a pail,
And then her mum would quickly guess,
That she would spill it down her dress.
Then think of how the tea would taste!
I feel it would have been a waste.
And then the cow might drink it first,
Leaving Mary with a thirst.

The cow in the field,
The milk in the tea;
I think that's how it ought to be!

Mary, Mary, quite contrary

Mary, Mary, quite contrary,
How does your garden grow?

By digging muck,
My silly duck,
And that you surely know!

Weedkiller you get from the chemist's,
and fertilizer, too;
You work and work,
and never shirk,
until your face is blue.

And, since you ask,
about my task,
to make my garden grow,
I prune and weed and irrigate,
and then there's grass to mow.

That's the secret of success,
in making my garden grow.

There was an old woman

There was an old woman who lived in a shoe.
She had so many children she must know what to do;
She made them rise early, for she was no fool,
Then washed their faces and sent them to school.